Egyptian Mythology

A Guide to Ancient Egyptian Religion, Beliefs, and History

DUSTIN YARC

The following book is reproduced below with the goal of providing information that is as accurate and as reliable as possible. The author does not claim to be an expert or scholar on the topics discussed within this work, and that any recommendations or suggestions made herein are for entertainment purposes only.

This declaration is deemed fair and valid by both the American Bar Association and the Committee of Publishers Association and is legally binding throughout the United States.

Furthermore, the transmission, duplication or reproduction of any of the following work, including precise information, will be considered an illegal act, irrespective whether it is done electronically or in print. The legality extends to creating a secondary or tertiary copy of the work or a recorded copy and is only allowed with express written consent of the Publisher. All additional rights are reserved.

The information in the following pages is broadly considered to be a truthful and accurate account of facts, and as such any inattention, use or misuse of the information in question by the reader will render any resulting actions solely under their purview. There are no scenarios in which the publisher or the original author of this work can be in any fashion deemed liable for any hardship or damages that may befall them after undertaking information described herein.

Additionally, the information found on the following pages is intended for informational purposes only. As befitting its nature, the information presented is without assurance regarding its continued validity or interim quality. Any trademarks that are mentioned are done without written consent and can in no way be considered an endorsement from the trademark holder.

DEDICATION

To my elementary school teacher, Mrs Hines,
who inspired much of my interest in ancient Egypt.

CONTENTS

INTRODUCTION

Congratulations on purchasing your personal copy of Egyptian Mythology. Thank you for doing so.

The following chapters will discuss many aspects of Egyptian mythology and the overall beliefs of the ancient Egyptians, as well as historical information about Egyptian culture at the time.

You will learn lots of great information about topics such as:

- The Gods and Goddesses of ancient Egypt
- Ancient Egyptian Creation Myths
- Death and The Afterlife, as understood by ancient Egyptians
- Maat, the Egyptian concept of morality and order
- Religious customs and burial beliefs of ancient Egypt
- A look at ancient Egyptian society, including their daily lives and their technology, medicine, and science.
- The ultimate legacy of ancient Egypt
- As well as many other amazing thing from ancient Egyptian history and mythology.

There are plenty of books on this subject on the market, thanks again for choosing this one! Every effort was made to ensure it is full of as much useful information as possible. Please enjoy!

PART ONE: MYTHOLOGY AND RELIGION

The land of Egypt has tantalized the minds of countless generations. The mysterious oasis along the mighty Nile River has been seen as a cradle of civilization and has captured the public imagination. Yet, the general populace knows very little about the people whose Kings and even Queens are household names. Those with a tenuous grasp on Egyptian history and culture know even less about their extensive worldview, mythologies, and religious rites.

Egyptian history is unique in and of itself but can be easily compared with Indo-European and Abrahamic religion throughout history and into the modern day. It can be argued that as a cradle of civilization, Egyptian lore has fundamentally influenced our worldview in the modern west.

1 GODS AND GODDESSES

While Egypt eventually did become one of the great centers of Christianity, with the city of Alexandria being part of the Pentarchy, the ancient Egyptians in the pre-Christian era were devoutly polytheistic. They believed in a pantheon of Gods and Goddesses and possessed a worldview wholly unique to themselves and the land that they lived on. It could, in fact, be argued that Egyptian culture could only have evolved along the Nile River.

Groups of people are shaped by the environments in which they live and develop their cultural values. The land of Egypt is one of polarity – scorching hot deserts juxtaposed with fertile oases along the river. The lives of the early Egyptians were ruled by the daily cycles of sunrise and sunset and the yearly cycles of floods and drains. The concepts of endless death and rebirth appear throughout Egyptian myth and folklore, and their deities were by no means an exception to this mode of thought.

RA

Throughout polytheistic religion, there is invariably a high God or Goddess. The Egyptians were no exception. The power of the sun decided the fate of the Egyptian people just as much as the Nile's yearly floods did. Thus, it was only natural that their highest God should be a God of the Sun. The themes of death and rebirth extended to and emanated from Ra. Each day, he rose in his chariot in the glorious sunrise, and each night died and descended into the underworld to fight off otherworldly dangers with the help of warrior deities. Ra, like the sun with which his name is explicitly identified, was seen as the creator of the entire world and the King of the

Gods.

Ra's association with Kingship extended to Egyptian society. Due to the actions of man and the mercy of the high God, the Pharaoh was considered to be the representative of Ra on Earth. As Ra was the creator of all things, the source of all life and death through his association with the sun, and both the king and ultimate father of both man and divine beings, his rule was law. Those in whom Ra had invested his favor were viewed as extensions of the God Himself. Often, they would be seen as a descendent of the high God or as an avatar of his descendant Horus. Whether this concept came about as a political or a purely theological concept is up for debate.

The Egyptians shared the idea of an overarching cosmic order with many other cultures, including the Abrahamic faiths and the Indo-Europeans. This overarching order, called maat, was considered by the Egyptian people to not only be the ideal through which the universe and society ought to operate, but as a divine law unto itself instituted by Ra who created all things.

While the Egyptians were decidedly polytheistic in their theology, they did have monistic tendencies when it came to Ra. Ra was the creator of the universe, and he himself was an uncreated being. In this guise as the creator, all beings were thus seen as emanations or even parts of Ra. An epithet for Ra was "the one from whom came millions."

Other deities were identified with the sun and creator aspects later on in Egyptian history, most especially Amun. However, his cult did not gain widespread acceptance until he was syncretized with Ra, becoming Amun-Ra. Ra was depicted as a man with the head of a falcon, crowned with the sun holding an ankh representative of his eternal nature.

AMUN

The early Egyptians may have had monistic tendencies, but were polytheists in every other sense. Amun represented a gradual shift towards monotheism, while still maintaining a culture of acceptance towards old theologies.

Amun, especially after his identification with Ra, was seen as the ultimate creator deity containing all aspects of prior gods and goddesses within him. He even took on the epithet of Ra: the one from whom came millions. Because he had taken on the monistic aspects of Ra, the worship of other deities was seen as in effect the worship of Amun, allowing for religious pluralism and tolerance within Egyptian society. Amun is unique among

Egyptian gods in that he is often depicted entirely in human form, with no anthropomorphized aspects from other animals. This may be reflective of the changing Egyptian concept of deity from the forces of the natural world outside of their control to a being intimately connected with their humanity and human ingenuity.

OSIRIS

Few myths are better known from the Egyptian narratives than that of Osiris. This may be due to the parallels found within it to other death and resurrection tales, chiefly that of the Christ myth. Osiris, the son of Geb, was meant to be the king of the gods after Ra (later Amun-Ra) ceded the title. Seth, jealous of Osiris, brutally murdered him and scattered his body parts across Egypt. Bereaved, his wife Isis wandered the land in search of his pieces in an attempt to give him a proper burial. Through the events of this tale, his son Horus is conceived.

Osiris, as Lord of the Underworld, was deeply connected with the concepts of fertility, resurrection, immortality, and of course death. Osiris, as a being who was believed to bring those who came to him to their perfected state, was thought to merge at least in part with Ra as he traversed the underworld each night.

ISIS

Isis was the quintessential goddess of the Egyptian pantheon, much like Vesta, Hestia, or other hearth goddesses throughout the world. She was much beloved by women, as she embodied every aspect of a woman's life – from the joys of youth, the pangs of motherhood, to the deep grief of widowhood. She was also heavily associated with magic due to her role in the resurrection of Osiris.

Through her identification as the mother of Horus, Isis was often thought to be the protector of the Pharaoh – commonly seen as his incarnation. She soon became a Goddess responsible for a multitude of roles and was seen as something of a divine protectress. The title "Queen of Heaven," more commonly associated in modern times with the Virgin Mary, was an epithet applied to Isis during the height of her cult when she was adopted by both the Greeks and Romans.

HORUS

Horus was a deity most well known for his association with the Pharaoh. Not only was Horus the King of the Gods at the behest of Ra (or Amun-Ra in later myths), the Pharaoh was also granted similar authority over man and was seen by the Egyptian priesthood and public as the incarnation of Horus on Earth. While all of the Gods lived in an abode beyond the sky (see The Fall of Man), Horus was regarded as the embodiment and god of the   sky.

Horus was also considered a champion-like figure. Through his descent from Osiris, Horus claimed that he was the heir to the throne of the gods. He defeated his uncle Seth in every contest for it, demonstrating his superior nature to his murderous relation. This tale serves to prove to the Egyptian people the superiority and divine right of the Pharaoh when compared to the enemies of Egypt who are identified with Seth.

SETH

Seth, or Set, was a god of chaos in the Egyptian mythos. He is the destabilizing force, forcing change and the exchange of power from one generation to the next. Though he was the murderer of Osiris and a bringer of discord, Seth cannot be said to be a purely evil being. His immense strength was seen as invaluable to Ra, who used him as a divine guard during his nightly trips to the underworld against all those whom would harm him and end life in the universe as we know it, including the serpent Apophis.

Seth was commonly identified with the chaotic and deadly aspects of the natural world. He is the heat that bears down relentlessly upon your head as your traverse the endless deserts. He is the horrific and destructive storms. He is the bloodthirsty warrior that dismembers his enemies and throws their parts to the wind.

Yet, it is important to remember that sometimes destruction is necessary. The relentless sun also enables your crops to grow, the storms wash away old brush to make room for the new, and the berserk warrior is all that stands between the people and those that would harm them. Seth was an ambiguous figure, and his cult and anti-cults reflect that status.

Seth was unique in that his head, while animalistic, portrays no animal known to man in any coherent sense.

HATHOR

Hathor was a well-loved goddess among the Egyptian people. As a being responsible for joy and fertility, her cult was popular among women of all strata of society. She was often depicted as a cow or with the features of a cow, and was believed to be the cow separating the Earth from the divine (though in some versions of the tale this was actually the goddess Nut, wife of Geb). In some of her aspects, Hathor was viewed as the real mother of Horus.

Many of the elements traditionally associated with Hathor would later be fused with or outright supplanted by Isis as her cult grew in prominence.

PTAH

Ptah was one of the many sun gods that the Egyptians recognized, and was considered particularly important for the city of Memphis. In fact, in Memphite theology, this patron deity was the creator of the entire universe – not Ra. Ptah differed from Ra in that in the Memphite version of the creation myth, he created the universe through his spoken word (similar to the God of Abraham), and not his ejaculate. Ptah was seen as more personable than Ra, more willing to listen to the petitions of those who were devoted to him. This could help to explain his enduring popularity throughout Egyptian history.

ATUM

Atum was one of the many sun gods among the Egyptians, but he may have been one of the earliest before being supplanted by Ra. Atum and Ra become functionally the same being very early on in Egyptian history and are in effect the same being. Whenever a new deity rose to prominence, the Egyptians had no problems whatsoever with syncretizing their gods into one being. Later on, Ra and Amun would fuse into the being Amun-Ra.

KHEPRI

Khepri was yet another deity of the sun. Egyptian religion never had any focus on Orthodoxy outside of the reign of King Akhenaten. As such, it can be more accurately said that Egyptian religion was at times a collection of multiple different regionally associated faiths – similar to the situation found in modern day India.

When Khepri wasn't being used as a replacement for Ra or Atum in the creation myth, he was being placed into a sort of trinity with the other two sun deities. Within this trinity, Khepri was the morning sun, Ra the midday sun, and Atum the setting sun. This was visualized as Khepri rising like a scarab from the desert sands in the morning. Khepri himself was associated with the scarab, and the insects were viewed as inherently connected to him.

THOTH

Thoth was a deity that was considered to be the patron of scribes and learned people. He was a god of the moon, due to his association with the Egyptian lunar calendar which required extensive calculations and the direct scribe of the gods especially when it came to recording the results of the judgment of the dead. In some versions of the myths, Thoth rather than Osiris would pass judgment on the deceased soul.

Thoth was also known as a god of magic and was invoked nearly as often as Isis towards that end. This was due to his vast knowledge, rather than magical talent being innate to him as it was in the case of his female counterpart.

Where Seth was the protector of Ra, Thoth was the protector of Osiris. He rose to keep watch on humanity during the night with the moon and descended back into the underworld with it every morning. He was considered to be a close friend and companion to the lord of the dead. Alongside this, he was heavily associated with the goddess Maat and is named as her consort and husband in some versions of the text.

ANUBIS

Anubis was the protector of the dead and the deity that attended the weighing of one's heart against the feather of maat. Ultimately, he was the deity who would escort the soul of the dead Egyptian to their final destiny – whether that be the fields of the dead or annihilation in the maws of Ammit.

Anubis is portrayed in a rather interesting way. One of the primary reasons why the Egyptians began to mummify their dead was to protect the body from feral animals, most commonly canids. Anubis was portrayed with the head of a jackal or African golden wolf – both animals known for eating carrion left in the desert. This association may have been the catalyst for the creation of Anubis's role as the decider of men's fates.

Anubis, and by extension, the jackal were thought to be protectors of the tombs of the dead. Prayers to Anubis invoking his protection would be found inscribed in tombs or written on the bandages of the deceased. He would also be invoked during the embalming process, as it was said that he was the deity who created the process in the first place after the death of Osiris.

SEKHMET

Sekhmet was as terrifying as she was beloved. While she was considered to be a goddess associated with healing, she was much better known for her more destructive aspects. In the creation and fall of man narratives, Sekhmet was the daughter of Ra and was set upon humanity by her father during the height of his displeasure. Sekhmet nearly drove humanity to extinction and was only quelled when Ra poured red colored beer on the earth and got her so drunk that she completely forgot about obliterating humanity.

Sekhmet was considered to be a protectress and also a fearsome warrior. The lioness was the most feared and respected animal among the Egyptian people. They were viewed as the epitome of strength and power.

As such, Sekhmet was viewed as the personal protector of the Pharaoh, aiding him in battle and warfare. It should be noted that up until very late in Egyptian history, the outcome of wars were seen as the cyclical victories and defeats mirroring those of the gods. Later on, the prayers and rituals performed by the Pharaoh were seen as having the potential to influence the will of the divine and affect humanity's lot in life. This may have been an influence derived from contact with monotheistic religions that had a more linear view of time.

NUT

Depending on which version of the creation myth that you read, Nut was one of the first deities. The daughter of the air god Shu, she fell madly in love with her brother Geb, the god of the Earth. Shu wasn't pleased with this and raised Nut into the sky. He then placed himself between the two of them, keeping them forever separate.

GEB

Geb was the god of the Earth, and heavily associated with the benben, or the first land on which the god Ra stood on while he created the universe. Geb could be both benevolent and destructive: he, like Osiris, caused the crops to grow. Yet at the same time, his laughter would cause earthquakes – an especially deadly natural disaster during the ancient times. Geb was separated from his wife Nut at the behest of their father, Shu.

APOPHIS

Apophis, also known as Apep, was the serpent of primordial chaos. While the Egyptians did not have a definite conception of good and evil, they did view Apophis as an entity who personified evil. They feared Apophis to such a degree that the god Seth, a being associated with chaos in his own right, was assigned to defend Ra from Apophis as he traversed the underworld each night – lest Ra be consumed and the world end.

Apophis was not an object of worship. All rites performed towards him were towards the end of keeping him bound and the maat from being destroyed. He was often mutilated by worshippers in effigy in order to continually kill and bind him from causing harm to the world. Apophis can be compared to other great serpents of myth, including the beast from the Book of Revelation or the Midgard serpent from Norse lore.

NUN

Nun was the personification of the primordial waters that existed before the gods and before the very universe itself. The benben, or the first pyramid of earth, arose from the waters of Nun. Standing atop of the benben, Ra masturbated and from his ejaculate emerged the first gods and the   universe.

Nun had a chaotic aspect to her, and in later times this is what she was primarily identified with. Nun was an entirely transcendent concept or being. She existed outside of and before time. As such, she was not necessarily worshiped directly. As an entirely primordial being, she was not seen as being knowable or a personal or even corporate level. No temples were erected to Nun.

NEPHTHYS

Nephthys was one of the original primordial deities, and the daughter of Geb and Nut, sister of Osiris, Isis, and Seth. Nephthys was associated with death, rebirth, mummification, and guardianship over temples and the Pharaoh. As the wife of Seth, she played a central role in the Death of Osiris. Her son, Anubis, is thought to also be the son of Osiris and a divine counterpart to Horus, son of Osiris and Isis. In other versions of the myth, either she or Hathor are identified as the mother of Horus. The popularity of Isis eventually eclipsed that of Nephthys.

SHU

Shu was one of the first children of Ra, along with his sister and wife, Tefnut. He was identified as the primordial god of the air, and the father of Geb and Nut. Displeased with the relationship between his children, he forcibly raised Nut into the air and placed himself between her and Geb. From this act were formed the land and the sky, with the vast expanse of wind and air eternally separating them. This act also created the conditions by which mankind and physical reality were allowed to exist. The reunion of Geb and Nut had the potential to end the world.

TEFNUT

Where Shu was considered to be a dry influence, his wife Tefnut was the personification of moisture. The name Tefnut literally translates as "the waters." Tefnut had the head of a lioness, and could potentially be an early version of Sekhmet before this second daughter of Ra earned a cult in her own right. Tefnut did not have many centers of worship, and it is arguable as to whether she had a consistent cult at all. The few cult centers that she had existed in Heliopolis and Leontopolis.

IMHOTEP

Imhotep was an exceptionally unique deity. Unlike his compatriots, Imhotep did not exist at the creation of the universe nor did he claim descent from a deity. He was instead a commoner who served King Djoser as the high priest of Ra. Imhotep's mother was a human being, but his later deification allowed him to become the son of Sekhmet and Ptah. He was considered to be such a great physician and philosopher that after his death he became a deity in his own right. The tomb of Imhotep has never been found, though not for lack of effort on the part of Egyptologists. The name Imhotep means "the one who comes in peace."

SOBEK

Sobek was one of the principle gods of the Nile River. Often portrayed with the head of a crocodile, he is yet another example of the Egyptians anthropomorphizing creatures that are otherwise extremely dangerous into a more protective figure (see Anubis). The god Sobek was invoked to keep Egyptians safe from crocodiles and other animals as they sailed up and down the Nile. He also had fertility and war like aspects, depending on the version of the myth that one reads.

BASTET

Bastet, also known as Bast, was one of the possible predecessors of Sekhmet in some regions of Egypt. She was a warrior sun goddess with the head of a cat, and was thought to be one of the principal deities fighting against Apophis. Bastet was also seen as a mother goddess.

The deity was heavily associated with cats, which were sacred to the ancient Egyptians. Cats were revered for their hunting prowess when it came to vermin, and were thought to be the guardians of the underworld. It was illegal to kill a cat in Egypt – if one came across a dead cat, they would have to immediately proclaim that they were not the ones who had slain the animal. If a family cat died, Egyptians would often shave their eyebrows off in   mourning.

This reverence to cats extended to when they died. Beloved cats were often mummified with their masters. Thousands of cat mummies have been found in cultic centers sacred to the goddess Bastet, along with scores of the animals appearing in the tombs of Pharaohs, nobility, wealthy people, and even peasants.

KEK

Kek was a frog-headed deity from some versions of the ogdoad, or original eight deities. While primarily seen as male, Kek was viewed as a god with both a male and female aspect representing both night and day. The deity was meant to personify the primordial chaos from whence the universe first arose.

Kek has seen a modern resurgence as a cultic figure in some circles on the internet.

2 STORIES

Like any polytheistic culture, the ancient Egyptians did not draw their central beliefs from a holy book like the Bible, Torah, or Quran. Instead, they drew their theological concepts and advice for daily living from their legends and other sacred narratives passed down through their oral, liturgical, and occasionally even written traditions. However, unlike other polytheistic cultures such as the Celtic and Norse peoples, the ancient Egyptians did not have a particularly large repertoire of tales, preferring instead to have a select few full of depth and meaning.

Storytelling is the means through which a culture transmits its history and values to the next generation. Rather than encapsulate their views in lengthy written treatises on philosophy and morality, it can instead be passed down through easily digestible tales and fables that even a small child could understand and absorb. Stories also have the advantage of being easily memorizable – an important skill to have if you're an ancient Egyptian priest.

CREATION MYTHS

The Egyptians can be considered unique among the ancient cultures of the world in that they did not have one creation myth but four. They do however retain similar themes known to Indo-European and even Semitic religious thought: order arising from chaos, flame or the sun rising or otherwise commingling with primal waters to create the holy powers. Ancient peoples relied on the establishment of a sense of order from the chaotic and oft deadly wilderness around them, and the Egyptians were no exception to this rule.

Up to four creation myths were prominent throughout the height and decline of Egypt. These myths did not necessarily conflict, even if they at times contradicted one other. Even during the rise of the monotheistic tendencies of the cult of Amun-Ra, Egyptian society remained largely polytheistic and religiously pluralistic. The differences in myth were simply seen as different expressions of the same cosmic truth.

This can be jarring for Westerners who study Egyptian myth. The influence of strong monotheism on Western cultural perceptions leads many to believe that there can only be one accepted truth among a culture. Any heterodoxy is at best a contradiction, at worst outright heretical. Polytheistic cultures did not have this influence, and as such did not have as many religiously motivated conflicts amongst themselves, then the latter monotheistic nation states that we have come to know.

The Heliopolis myth is one of the earliest that we know of, and is perhaps the myth from which all other iterations derive. It goes as follows:

In the beginning, there was nothing but the void. Within the void, there were the chaotic waters known as Nun. From the waters arose the god Ra, also known as Atum in some versions of the myth. This motif of fire arising out of primal, chaotic waters is not unique to the Egyptians. It can be seen in Norse, Hindu, and even latter Christian creation narratives, and perhaps derives from the life-giving properties of fire and water in the lives of early man.

Ra, or Atum, stood atop of the benben, a pyramid that had arisen out of the waters of Nun. He then proceeded to masturbate, and from his seed came the deities Shu (the god of the air) and the goddess Tefnut. They then produced their own children, including Geb (the God of the Earth), and Nut (the Goddess of the Sky).

From the divine spark came the air, associated in many traditions with enlightenment and the divine masculine, and the first spark of the divine feminine, often associated with deep thought and emotion. Their roles switch in their children, with the divine masculine taking on the role of the fertile Earth, and the divine feminine taking on the role of the sky which would one day become the lofty abode of the Gods.

Shu, the air, desired to end the relationship between Geb and Nut. Nut was then forced to reside high above Geb and become the firmament between the skies and the heavens. Shu then put himself between them, forever keeping his children away from one other. In some versions of the myth, the goddess Hathor (sometimes identified with Isis) was raised to become the sky instead of Nut.

The grandchildren of Shu and Tefnut were Osiris, Isis, Seth, and

Nephthys. These first deities were considered by many to be the creators of the cosmos and some of the most important in the entire Egyptian pantheon.

While the creation story of the Egyptians does have parallels to other mythos, it is unique in and of itself in that the Egyptian people considered creation to be a continuing and cyclical process. It did not bother the Egyptians on a spiritual level when a new deity's cult grew to prominence, as the gods were seen to be constantly procreating among themselves. Likewise, the cyclical nature of time itself was seen as a miniature creation story in and of itself.

Later creation myths would expand on the concepts first introduced in the Heliopolis myth, often through the addition of intermediary deities or introducing the intent of the divine forces into the tale.

Sometimes creation myths would be used to benefit certain cities, leaders, or religious factions. The creation myth would be altered in some cities, chiefly the likes of Memphis, in order to place local deities above the established pantheon and elevate their perceived importance in Egyptian society. An example of this would be the cities identification of their deity Ptah as the creator of Atum or Ra, rather than the established creator being an uncreated being as he was throughout the rest of Egypt. They did this to elevate their own chosen deity without having to completely rewrite the established theology that their denizens had already come to know. Due to the pluralistic nature of Egyptian religion, it was easy to accept Ptah as the new creator – especially since the rest of their creation myth had remained functionally identical. None of their prior gods and goddesses had to be erased; their position in the hierarchy had merely changed in a sometimes imperceptible way to the average lay worshipper. Even the priesthood of Memphis was able to adjust to the changes without much fuss.

Sectarianism in this form was prevalent throughout the ancient world. City states would look for a reason to elevate their patron god and continue its cult despite the religious pressures coming from outside of their immediate geography. The same pattern can be seen in India, ancient Rome, and Greece, though admittedly less so in the latter. What is key is that these lesser deities were almost exclusively worshiped locally, and had very small if not non-existent cults anywhere else.

To the Egyptians, the events of creation were both ongoing and outside of time. The initial creation took place before time itself was even created, and yet it continued in a cyclical pattern of birth, death, and rebirth. Much like the Nile flooded on a yearly basis, bringing life and vitality to an otherwise barren and desolate landscape, so too did the divine beings arise out of the primal waters and the light – so too did they die and be reborn.

This theme of life, death, and rebirth to glorious immortality can be seen again and again throughout Egyptian lore. The land shaped the people, and so the people shaped their mythos.

THE FALL OF MAN

Egyptian thought differs from the geographically nearby Indo-European current and aligns itself more closely with Semitic and Abrahamic lines of thought in its conception of humanity as a fallen race. Much like the events familiar to most Westerners as detailed in Genesis, the Egyptians viewed their state in life as a consequence of humanity's collective rebellion against the divine will and the cosmos. This concept also serves as a convenient explanation of the nigh unlimited power of the Pharaoh in Egyptian society.

Before the onset of time, humanity lived in harmony with the divine, ruled over by Ra. Evil, which the Egyptians thought of as innate to the human condition and to the chaotic state of the universe itself before the establishment of cosmos by the Gods, seeped into this utopian world.

Humanity made the decision to attempt to overthrow the gods and their creator. The reasons behind this were not made explicitly clear in the text. This motif is common to myths that attempt to postulate why the divine and mortal beings are separate from one other. Where it differs from other myths, most especially the Abrahamic current is in two ways: it takes place in a time outside of time as we know it, and evil was not introduced to man through their actions.

The problem of evil is a difficult one in religious studies, and one which the modern monotheistic faiths continually struggle with. To the Egyptians, evil was just another part of the concept of chaos – the primordial darkness that existed before the gods and goddesses established order.

While the fall of man is used by the Abrahamic faiths to explain the concepts of death and divine punishment, it was utilized by the Egyptians to explain the established political order. Like other ancient polytheisms, it was at times tough to separate religion from politics and culture.

Ra felt that humanity was to be punished for their rebellion. As such, he set the lion Goddess Sekhmet upon them to bathe in their blood. Rather than destroy his creation completely, however, Ra satiated Sekhmet with red colored beer at the height of her carnage. Then, he separated Hathor (or Nut) from the god Geb by raising her into the skies, placing the god Shu between her and Geb. In the creation mythos, Shu did this of his own volition. However, due to the pluralistic nature of Egyptian religion, these contradictions do not need to conflict.

Ra then placed his representative, or in some versions of the text Horus himself, upon the Earth in the form of the Pharaoh. Thus, while humanity was separated from the divine due to their own rebellion, they were still ruled over by their divine king through his son (or grandson). Because of this, the proverbial church and the state could not possibly be separated. To anger the Pharaoh was to anger or offend the representative of the creator and a deity in his own right. Obedience to the Pharaoh was thus submission to maat, or the divine natural order. This institution was thought to have been put in place by the creator to curtail man's natural inclination towards evil, war, and endless bloodshed.

The Egyptians did have the concept of sin resulting from these events, but not in the same sense as the Abrahamic faiths. Sin did not separate humanity from the transcendent divine; the actions of primordial man had already done so. Instead, they weighed down the heart and increased one's chances of being denied entry into the afterlife and ultimate union with the divine. To sin was to act in ways that were contrary to maat – the natural order.

THE DEATH OF OSIRIS

If there is any tale from the Egyptian mythos well known to the public at large, it is almost certainly that of the Death of Osiris. Osiris was the son of the god Geb, who was the son of Shu and the grandson of Ra. As kingship was passed down through the paternal line, it thus passed to Osiris. He ruled over an era of peace, but aroused the ire of his brother Seth. Seth then proceeded to murder his brother, and scatter his parts across the land of Egypt.

The sister, and wife, of Osiris (Isis) searched far and wide for the body of her husband. Her plight was seen as so horrific that the wife of Seth, Nephthys, was moved to help her sister to collect the body parts of her husband. Eventually, Isis was able to find and reassemble the body of Osiris, and wrap him in bandages in order to keep him together.

Isis was considered to be a goddess associated with marriage, but even she couldn't bring Osiris back to life. Instead, she whispered one of the names of Ra into the ear of her husband, which brought him to life just long enough to impregnate Isis with the true heir to the throne of the gods. Osiris then went into the underworld, where he assumed kingship there.

Isis gave birth to Horus and raised him in secret. When he was old enough, he went to challenge Seth for the kingship. The council of the gods agreed that as the son of Osiris, he was the rightful king. Ra, however, did not. The mother of Ra decided that Horus ought to be the king, and gave Seth some of Ra's daughters as payment for what had been taken from him.

The arguments continued and culminated in Isis being forced to leave the court. She returned in disguise, and pleaded with Seth as a king to return to her son what he had been cheated of. Not realizing who it was, Seth pronounced a judgment in her favor: giving up his own kingship in the process. He then challenged Horus to multiple contests, which included but were not limited to events such as Isis's decapitation and resurrection, Seth being forced to eat lettuce with Horus's semen on it, and Seth creating a stone boat which promptly sank. Horus won every contest, and thus gained the kingship.

Compounding on all of this, Osiris sent a letter filled with threats from the Underworld if his son was not granted his kingship. Seth was made the protector of Ra in the underworld, and Horus reigned over an era of extreme prosperity.

The Death of Osiris is the story on which the political establishment of ancient Egypt was founded. The kingship was both eternal and patriarchal. It was passed from father to son in the form of the endless drama of death and rebirth through the story of Horus and Osiris. When a Pharaoh passed away, he became Osiris – descending into the divine underworld. At that exact moment, his son would instantly become the incarnation of Horus upon the Earth. It is possible that the Egyptian people viewed this on a more metaphysical level, but it is also clear from their writings and their cultural practices that they viewed the Pharaoh as a literal god on Earth.

It is interesting that challenges to the throne are identified with Seth in this legend. While Seth himself is not necessarily an evil being, he was heavily identified with chaos and the forces contrary to maat. It was said that any person who acted in accordance with isfet (chaos) rather than the established divine order (maat) had the spirit of Seth residing within them. Any being who acted contrary to maat, contrary to the established political order, were easily discredited through this tale. This led to an astoundingly long-lived political institution when viewed through the long view of history.

3 CONCEPTS

ANCIENT EGYPTIAN THEOLOGY

The Egyptians were a polytheistic people, as much of the ancient world before them. At the same time, they also had monistic and even monotheistic tendencies.

The Egyptians were a religiously pluralistic society in that none of these views conflicted to the degree that they would bring about iconoclasm or religiously motivated warfare, outside of a few isolated incidents.

In the time before time, there was nothing but chaos. From the chaotic, primordial waters, arose the sun god (Ra, Amun, Ptah). It was from this first divine being that all other deities and beings proceeded. In this way, the Egyptians were monistic. All things proceeded from one single source. While the Gods may have been viewed as distinct beings in their own right, each one of them contained a piece of the Supreme Being within them.

Local cults could also be henotheistic, meaning that while they recognized the existence of other deities, they viewed them as lesser beings or ultimately unimportant to their daily lives. The mythology could even be edited in order to serve the political classes of the local cult. This can be seen especially in the case of the Memphite theology surrounding the god Ptah and his usurpation of the role of the Supreme from Ra.

Religion and the political establishment were intertwined to the point that they could not be reasonably separated. The right of the Pharaoh to rule came from the Creator, and as King, he was the representative of the divine on Earth to rule in his stead. At many points in Egyptian history, this went further – with the Pharaoh being seen as the literal incarnation of Horus and the ultimate authority over both God and Man. The decrees of the Pharaoh were literally the decrees of the Divine. Thus, to oppose the State in any way was to be in direct opposition to the Divine and to maat, the natural cosmic order.

While the Gods and Goddesses were transcendent, residing in a realm beyond the sky, they were not totally absent from the world and would often intervene in its affairs directly. They were not lofty, unreachable beings. Key deities would control every aspect of the natural world. The Gods were the keepers of order throughout the entire universe, and their total absence would be the prelude to an utter collapse of all of reality.

Strict monotheism only arose in limited circumstances throughout the history of Egypt, chief among them being Akhenaten's cult of the god Aten. The cult of Aten was exclusive, as will be expounded on in the following section.

AKHENATEN'S RELIGIOUS REVOLUTION

Henotheism is the belief that while other deities exist, they are largely unimportant when compared to one's personal, familial, or local patron deity. The concept can be seen even in the earliest histories of the world's monotheisms, with references to other deities being rife throughout the Old Testament and the Torah. Henotheism can and does thrive in polytheistic environments, but tends to be a prelude to strict monotheism once it infiltrates the political classes.

This is exactly what happened when Akhenaten ascended the Egyptian throne. Aten, or the sun disk crown worn by Ra and later the growing cult of Amun, had become a patron deity in its own right to the royal family. However, they continued to worship Ra, and then Amun-Ra, in public due to the religious nature inherent to the nature of the monarchy. Their position was a result of the grace of the creator, and to fail to worship him in accordance with maat would threaten their office.

Akhenaten viewed the sun as the sole source of divine power. Aten, represented by the solar disk, was intentionally pushed in such a way that other deities first lost their power, and then their right to exist in Egyptian society. Aten was the creator and sustainer of all things. There could be no other partners. If Aten was the sole sustainer, then what power could other deities possibly have? Why did they then have the right to exist alongside the Most High? The cult Akhenaten had created could not tolerate the previous pluralism inherent to Egyptian religion – it sought only to destroy it and leave itself as the sole religious force in the land. Aberrant religious expression was aggressively routed and destroyed under the rule of Akhenaten.

This, of course, brought into question the legitimacy of the office of the

King. After all, if the authority of the King came from Amun-Ra in accordance with maat, and Amun-Ra was a false god, from whence did the power of the Pharaoh flow?

Akhenaten sought to answer this question in a way that took the concept of a divine king to its logical conclusion. Akhenaten convinced the Egyptian people that he had been placed on Earth by Aten Himself in order to rule them and uphold maat. Aten was viewed as fully transcendent from this reality, with the only exception to this being the Pharaoh. The King, as God's representative, was the only one who could fully comprehend and experience God. As such, worship of the King was the only way that the average people could (indirectly) worship God. Shrines to the King were ordered to be placed in every home, and replace the prior shrines to the old gods and goddesses.

The cult of Aten did not last. As soon as he died, the Egyptians went back to worshipping the old pantheon before his body was even in the ground. It was only the fear inspired by Akhenaten's inquisitorial regime that upheld the cult of Aten.

DEATH AND THE AFTERLIFE

The ancient Egyptians lived for their eventual deaths. This did not come from any disdain for their lives, quite the contrary. The Egyptians viewed life as a fundamentally good thing and desired nothing more than for the goodness of life to continue and increase in their afterlives. The afterlife was seen as both a continuation and an idealistic version of this one.

The road to the afterlife was a treacherous process. Egyptians would be given, during their life and at the time of their burial, a copy of "The Book of the Dead." Contained within this book were all of the instructions and procedures they would need to know in order to reach paradise.

Once they reached the underworld, known as Duat, they would be brought before Osiris, the lord of the dead. At this time, they would read a passage from the Book of the Dead detailing the terrible deeds, or sins, that they had not committed during their life. This was standard procedure, and did not affect their final outcome.

Whether or not a deceased individual could enter paradise was dependent on their final judgment. Their heart would be removed and weird against the feather of maat. The feather of maat represented the whole of the natural order of the universe. If one's heart weighed more than the feather of maat, they would be denied entry into paradise.

Those who were denied entry into paradise did not go to Hell as westerners conceive of the concept. Instead, they were consigned to a far worse fate. The monster Ammit stood next to the scales, ready to devour anyone who came to the court of Duet with a heart weighed down by sins. Those were consumed were traditionally considered to have been utterly destroyed.

The lucky ones whose hearts were lighter than the feather of maat were greeted with a life of pure bliss and vitality. The self was conceived of by the Egyptians as having a multitude of parts. This enabled the deceased Egyptian to exist on multiple different planes at once. One part of themselves became united with Osiris. All of their needs in Osiris's kingdom were met in abundance, and depending on their degree of wealth they would even be treated to supernatural servants to do their daily work for them. At the same time, they would also be united with Ra as he made his daily journey across the world. The dead who were granted entry into paradise were also granted union with the gods themselves. For a culture that saw themselves as fundamentally separated from the divine, this would have been seen as quite the reward indeed.

MAAT – MORALITY AND COSMIC ORDER

Few concepts were as central to the ancient world as that of a natural cosmic order. The concept of natural law was inherent to the ancient polytheisms. One worshiped the gods because that was part of the cosmic order – it was simply what you were meant to do. A modern equivalent, though not exact by any means, would be the concept of dharma from the Indian subcontinent. Maat stood in opposition to the concept of isfet, or primordial chaos.

Similarly to Christianity, the world at the beginning was one in which maat was perfected. There was no chaos, and everything was sustained perfectly by the divine. The actions of humanity then caused maat to be ruptured in the universe. The gods, unable to stomach a world where isfet was allowed to proliferate, thus left for their own abode where maat remained perfected.

This did not mean that isfet ruled the world, merely that it had more sway and would influence the nature of man to inherently rebel against maat. Maat remained in the natural order: the floods and receding of the Nile, the rising and setting of the sun, and most importantly in the rule of the Pharaoh as the representative of Ra. Obeying the Pharaoh was seen as submission to the divine, and by extension following maat. Moreover, acting in ways that were socially and culturally appropriate were other means of living in accordance with maat in its perfected state.

Isfet was said to dwell in people who acted in unsociable or individualistic behavior. In a social order where obedience is everything, part of the natural law of the universe, acting in nonconformist ways could have devastating consequences. On a physical level, it could lead to a failure of the crops or the deaths of your immediate kin group. On a metaphysical level, though, acting under the influence of Seth (said to be the ruler of isfet) could arouse the wrath of the gods. Angry deities could bring natural disaster, plague, or even conquering armies. Obedience to maat wasn't just being a good, decent human being: it had real life and death consequences.

Obeying maat would follow you into the next life. Those who obeyed the natural law would be admitted into paradise and ultimate union with the divine. Those who did not on the other hand, those who allowed isfet to influence their daily lives, would be devoured by Ammit and face complete annihilation. The consequences of disobedience were real to the Egyptians.

Like other concepts or natural processes, maat was also a personified being. The goddess Maat was thought to be the wife of Ra, and one of the first beings arising from creation. Her principle function was to uphold maat, the concept for which she was named. As part of this function, she was said to be the ultimate advisor to the Pharaoh. In fact, Pharaohs would often wear pendants depicting Maat as a means of making this function and their ultimate role as dispensers of maat more explicit.

TIME – NEHEH AND DJET

The way in which a culture sees the passage of time can tell one an awful lot about how they see the world overall. The Egyptians saw time in two ways –Neheh and Djet. There are no real approximations in English for these concepts. In that sense, they are much like maat and isfet.

Neheh is the cyclical nature of time. The sun rises and sets each day, and the Nile floods and recedes every year. Time was seen as cyclical and inexhaustible. Everything came full circle, and would continue to do so throughout the ages. Neheh was a view shared with a multitude of ancient cultures, and is in stark contrast to the Abrahamic conception of linear time.

Djet was more associated with the realm of the dead. It represented the culmination and completion of beings at the end of their ultimate destiny. The dead in paradise would remain in this exalted state for all time. Everything the Egyptians did in regards to funerals was with the concept of Djet in mind – it was all to keep things and people in their final state of exaltation for all time. Djet and Neheh would, interestingly enough, fuse during the night as Ra journeyed into the underworld. This ultimately represented the fact that life was eternal – that all beings that were worthy would be "reborn" in the realms of the dead just as the sun rose from the horizon every morning.

The Egyptian people, by and large, did not recognize history as a concept. Time was either a cycle or a permanent state of exaltation. They did not view history as something worthy of study if it did not pertain to the cycles ordained by maat or get them closer to their perfected afterlives. It was not until much later in Egyptian history, possibly after contact with monotheistic peoples, that any significance was applied to events whatsoever.

THE KA, THE BA, AND THE PARTS OF THE SELF

The Egyptians had a markedly different conception of the self than a modern westerner would. Modern people view the self in multiple ways, but the general underlying theme is that regardless of whether or not the self stems from the immaterial soul or electrical signals in the brain, the self is fundamentally one being. It wasn't so to the Egyptians. They viewed the self as being comprised of many different parts, which included the name, physical body, and two ethereal elements known as the ka and the ba. Each conception of the self existed both at once within the living person and independently in their dualistic conception of time and space.

The ka can be compared with the fundamental vitality of the self; it is the animating force that transcends time. Ka was an inherited trait from one's family, and remained even after the physical death. Ka was associated heavily with Djet; it was unchanging and eternal. The ka remained in the tomb after a person had died, leading in part to the unique customs of leaving grave goods found especially in the cases of royalty.

One's ka was also their social self. The memory of the person that lived on after their death was a form of life in and of itself. As such, those who were still remembered and spoken on in fond terms after their earthly demise could actually be considered as remaining in a living state in a certain sense of the word. Conversely, one could still be very much alive on the physical level, and yet for all intents and purposes dead on the societal level.

Your ba, on the other hand, could be considered as being your soul in a loose comparison of the word to the western concept of the word. The ba was your personality in a spiritual form. Even the gods and goddesses had bas, which enabled them to inhabit their idols here on Earth during worship services. The Egyptians did not worship the idol. Instead, they worshiped the ba of the deity that took up residence inside of the idol during the service. Once the service was over, the ba of the deity would leave. After death, the ba of the worthy human being would leave in much the same way in order to join Osiris in the underworld and Ra on his daily chariot ride.

Ka and ba would extend to the deities themselves. Identity was loose and an ever changing concept. It only existed to the Egyptians as side effects of the social relationships between beings whether they be divine or mortal. This enabled the Egyptians to seamlessly syncretize and merge deities when they rose or fell from prominence. They would simply begin to see them as ba and ka of one other. Eventually, they would fuse into a singular, complete deity in their own right. In some ways, this conception was a genius way of allowing for a religion that can continually grow and evolve without establishing a set orthodoxy.

ANCIENT EGYPTIAN COSMOLOGY

The cosmology (or way of seeing the world) of the ancient Egyptians was one that was fundamentally based upon the concept of maat. Maat was the divine cosmic order, and remained under constant threat from the forces of isfet, or disorder. This is similar to the other ancient polytheisms, and can be most closely compared with the concepts of dharma and adharma from the Indian subcontinent.

Maat was upheld by the divine forces and through right action on the part of mankind. Egyptians would worship and offer to the divine powers as a way of sustaining them in order for maat to be continually upheld. It was believed that if the gods were allowed to diminish, then isfet would overrun the universe and end it as human beings knew it.

To the Egyptians, the world was a flat sentient being: the god Geb. Geb was separated from his wife, the goddess Nut, who was the sky personified by their father: the god Shu who represented the air. Beyond Nut lived the Gods in their celestial home. The underworld was viewed similarly, with the primordial chaos goddess Nun making up the "undersky."

The Pharaoh, though thought to be a deity in his own right, was viewed as the representative of the creator on Earth. The world of the Pharaoh was law, and to disobey the Pharaoh was to go as far as to be in opposition to maat. Disobedience to the Pharaoh threatened the very balance of the cosmos.

RELIGIOUS CUSTOMS AND BURIAL BELIEFS

The Egyptians were a deeply religious people, but it should be noted that culture and politics could not be neatly separated from religion. This can seem foreign to modern westerners and their conception of the separation of church and state. Religion is viewed in modern times as something that ought to be separate from one's daily life. The Egyptians, on the other hand, lived their religious faith.

The Egyptians lived for their eventual deaths. They knew with the same certainty that the sun would rise every morning that they would one day be judged based on their adherence to the principles of maat. This judgment would decide the ultimate fate of their eternal selves.

These beliefs caused the Egyptian people to develop incredibly elaborate funerary rites. The belief that one's ka remained with the body even after death pushed the Egyptians to develop their methods of mummification. They believed that the person was still fundamentally present within their corpse – to allow them to decompose was akin to sacrilege. Depending on the area, the condition of one's ka could affect the condition of their ba in the afterlife. This belief was common among grave robbers, who would smash the faces of their victims in order to render them unrecognizable to the gods in the afterlife.

The need for preservation extended to the internal organs. During the mummification process, all of the organs save for the heart would be removed from the body and placed within miniature sarcophagi with the image of the deity most associated with that organ on it. The heart was left in purposefully so that it could be removed and weighed against the feather of maat in the court of Osiris. The brain was famously removed through the nose and discarded as waste material.

After the body was totally eviscerated, the process of dehydration would begin. The body would be left in a pile of special salts for a predetermined period of time. Once the body was totally dehydrated, it would be wrapped in linens and buried according to the social status of the person to whom it belonged. Poor Egyptians would receive a comparably poor mummification and would be left buried in the desert with what few grave goods their families could spare. Pharaohs, on the other hand, would be afforded elaborate and often booby-trapped tombs.

Once the body was sufficiently embalmed, a priest would be summoned to ceremonially "open the mouth" of the deceased. The spells spoken over the body would allow the person to speak and move in the next life. If these rites weren't performed, it was believed that the individual would be incapable of defending themselves in Osiris's court – let alone get there in the first place.

Like many other cultures, the Egyptians held to a rudimentary form of ancestor veneration. The spirits of the dead were believed to join Ra on his daily chariot rides across the skies. Thus, much like the saints of Catholic lore, they were thought to be able to intercede on behalf of their living family members. According to some versions of the myths, the dead could help their families directly under their own merits and power due to the perfected state inherent to the underworld.

It was believed that those who were buried improperly would become furious with their living family. Those who did not receive a proper burial would be unable to enter paradise, and would, therefore, return to wreak havoc on their living relations.

Egyptians were almost universally buried with a copy of The Book of the Dead. The Book of the Dead was a collection of spells, incantations, and procedures that the deceased would require in order to successfully traverse the underworld and gain entry into paradise. The Book of the Dead was not a standardized volume, and it didn't even need to necessarily be presented to the deceased in the form of a bound volume. It could be found inscribed onto the coffin, written on one's bandages, or even sprawled on the walls of one's tomb if the deceased was wealthy enough to afford it. The Book of the Dead was personalized for each individual in order to make the performance of the rights contained within it easier for the dead individual. The spells included could even be personalized at the request of the dead person, but this was only done in the cases of extraordinarily wealthy and learned individuals. The average person would not have the knowledge necessary to pick their own funerary spells.

PART TWO: THE HISTORY AND CULTURE OF THE ANCIENT EGYPTIANS

Egypt as a civilization has had a profound effect on the course of history and how we look at it in the modern day. The influence of the ancient Egyptians extended long past their fall and continues to tantalize us to this very day.

4 THE AGES OF EGYPT: PRE-DYNASTIC, EARLY DYNASTIC, OLD KINGDOM, MIDDLE KINGDOM, NEW KINGDOM AND DEMISE

Egyptian history can be separated into multiple different ages, all with their own flavor, major struggles, religious developments, and even architectural styles.

The pre-dynastic period of Egypt occurred prior to 3100 BC. Pre-historic peoples settled the Nile valley, and began transforming the land to suit their own needs. Several cultures emerged and fell during this period. Over two thousand years, these cultures conglomerated into two kingdoms: Upper Egypt and Lower Egypt. Upper Egypt existed to the south, and Lower Egypt to the north. These kingdoms were so named due to their proximity to the Mediterranean Sea, which the Nile eventually drains out into.

In the year 3150 BC, the king Menes unified both kingdoms into a single, united Egypt. This change can even be reflected in Egyptian artworks depicting the king; the crown became a fusion of the crowns of Upper and Lower Egypt. This Pharaoh is thought to have founded the first dynasties of Egypt, and is largely responsible for unifying and stabilizing Egyptian culture.

The early dynastic period lasted up until the third dynasty, founded in 2686 BC. This period of time, from the third dynasty to the sixth dynasty, is known to Egyptologists as the Old Kingdom period. This period is especially notable since the majority of pyramids were constructed during this time frame. The Pyramid of Djoser, also known as the Step Pyramid, was built during this time at Memphis. The Pyramid of Djoser is widely believed to be the earliest known pyramid construction in Egypt, and was constructed during the lifetime of King Djoser.

Pyramids were built as elaborate temples to the king, who was believed to be a deity in his own right. It was believed that the ka of a person remained after their death, and would continue to inhabit their tomb along with their corpse. Because the ka was the social aspect of a person, the pyramids were seen as a means of keeping the Pharaoh alive in a manner of speaking long after his demise. The end of pyramid destruction was mainly due to practicality. Though the constructions were booby trapped and at times even cursed, this did not sufficiently deter grave robbers. The pyramids served as enormous beacons to where great wealth was concentrated. These constructions were abandoned in favor of underground tomb burials, especially in the Valley of the Kings.

The Old Kingdom was brought to an end largely due to natural disasters and a succession struggle after the death of the Pharaoh Pepi II Neferkare. Famine and political infighting followed for over two hundred years.

The Middle Kingdom arose out of this period of chaos, and lasted from 2030 to 1650 BC, from the eleventh dynasty to the thirteenth. This period saw the capital moved from the city of Thebes to Lisht. It was known largely for extensive military campaigns against Egypt's neighbors, and intermittent stints of civil war. By the end of this period, the population growth of Egypt had begun to exceed their food creation capacities, leading to even more strife.

The New Kingdom saw the end of the foreign Hyksos rule in Egypt, and more extended military campaigns in an attempt to keep the nation from being conquered again. Pharaohs of this period included Hatshepsut, Ramesses I, II, and III, Psamtik I, and the Ptolemy dynasty. The Ptomelic dynasty was Greek in origin, but adopted Egyptian culture as their own – including incestuous marriage. The last Ptolemy Pharaoh was Cleopatra, Her various love affairs with Mark Antony and Octavian eventually led to her eventual assassination or suicide, depending on the source. Her death, on August 12, 30 BC marked the end of dynastic rule in Egypt. The nation was annexed and became a Roman province.

5 GOVERNMENT AND ECONOMY: LEGAL SYSTEM, SOCIAL STATUS, AGRICULTURE, NATURAL RESOURCES AND TRADE

The ancient Egyptians were decidedly a monarchy. Those at the top were believed to be divine themselves, or having been appointed to their position by the gods and goddesses. Chief among these figures were the Pharaoh, who was viewed as the literal incarnation of the god Horus. At the time of his death, he became identified with Osiris.

Society was shaped like a pyramid, with the divine at the top and the average person at the very bottom. Directly below the royal family were the government officials and priests. Below them, in descending order of importance, were the military, scribes, merchants, artisans, farmers, and finally slaves. The Egyptians had no qualms whatsoever about slavery, and believed it to be a divine institution. Wealth was continually transferred from the bottom to the top in accordance with the Egyptian belief in maat and the Pharaoh being himself a divine being. Giving gifts to the gods was part of the cosmic order, and this extended to the human beings put into their position by the divine. Taxes could be as high as 60 percent of one's harvest.

This did not mean that the average Egyptian farmer could expect to go hungry after paying their dues. The Nile was extraordinarily fertile. It was said that farmers would simply have to throw their seeds on the ground and wait after the yearly floods. Trade with their neighbors was common in the Old and early Middle Kingdoms. Later on, the Egyptians were more likely to attempt to conquer their neighbors through endless military campaigns rather than trade with them. Their overly expansive military eventually led in part to their downfall.

DUSTIN YARC

6 LANGUAGE: EGYPTIAN HIEROGLYPHS, SOUNDS AND GRAMMAR, WRITING AND LITERATURE

The Egyptian language, along with Sumerian, is one of the oldest written languages in the world. The language, now known as Coptic, is still spoken in a liturgical context in the Coptic Orthodox Church based primarily in Egypt.

A member of the Afro-Asiatic family, Egyptian went through multiple sound changes along with its neighbors until it's eventual decline and eradication in favor of Egyptian Arabic in the 17th century AD. The Semitic languages, themselves an offshoot of proto-Afro-Asiatic just like Egyptian, are the closest living languages to ancient Egyptian today with a stable amount of fluent speakers.

Egyptian is unique among world languages in that it has a three-vowel system: a, i, and u. They had voiced and pharyngeal consonants. The dialects of Egyptian correlated with the periods of Egyptian history, eventually culminating with Coptic until its eventual decline and demise. Prior to the creation of Coptic, dialectical differences did not matter in terms of written Egyptian. This is most similar to the Chinese languages, where the written language is centralized even if the spoken dialects do not have mutual intelligibility.

Egyptian hieroglyphs were separated into two classifications: ideograms, which represented pictorial representations of items and concepts, and phonograms, which most closely represented the sounds being created by the mouth when the word was spoken.

Hieroglyphs were known throughout Egypt by the learned class up until he 5th century AD. At that time, due in large part to the rise of Christianity and the changing laws and customs of the Roman Empire, all pagan temples throughout the now Roman province were permanently shuttered. Many stone tablets were also destroyed during this time.

Had it not been for the discovery of the Rosetta Stone in the year 1799, Egyptian writing would have remained indecipherable. Unlike the Romans or the Greeks, Egyptian writing did not have any immediate analog like their neighbors did with predecessor systems like Phoenician. The neighbors of the Egyptians did not use hieroglyphs, nor did they use anything even similar to them.

The Rosetta stone has the same story printed in three different scripts. These included ancient Egyptian hieroglyphs, demotic (another kind of Egyptian script more common to the pre-dynastic period and the Old Kingdom), along with ancient Greek. The presence of ancient Greek, which archaeologists and linguists already knew how to read, allowed Egyptologists to learn how to read Egyptian and thus translate all of the hieroglyphs that they had found. It further allowed linguists to reconstruct the Egyptian language throughout history. Because of how extensively ancient Egyptian was written down, linguists can successfully reconstruct the entire language going back to proto-Egyptian. At times, they can take this a step further and reconstruct proto-Afro-Asiatic with greater ease than linguists can construct other proto-languages like proto-Indo European.

Jean-Francois Champollion was the first person to completely translate the Rosetta stone, and did so by the year 1820.

7 CULTURE: DAILY LIFE, CUISINE, ARCHITECTURE, AND ART

Egyptian culture spanned over three thousand years, and remained remarkably stable throughout. In fact, the few attempts that there were to change Egyptian daily life, such as the reign of Akhenaten and his cult of Aten, backfired and never stuck. Egyptian religion did not change en masse until the introduction of Christianity to the city of Alexandria in 33 AD. By the year 300 AD, the city was a thriving Christian center and part of the Pentarchy. Pre-Christian polytheism persisted until the 5th century, at which time it was forcibly suppressed by the state, culminating in the shuttering of the temples. The modern Egyptian state is now 88% Muslim, with the religion largely being enforced by the state to the detriment of religious minorities.

Ancient Egyptian art was characteristically flat and non-proportional. Limbs were characteristically elongated, and all paintings were heavily stylized. Sculpture, on the other hand, presented a high degree of photorealism, consistent with their later Greco-Roman compatriots.

Figures were sized based on their hierarchy in society. The larger the figure, the more important they were. In any painting, the Pharaoh would be the largest figure of all. The Ptolemaic period, which occurred at the very end of the ancient Egyptian civilization, had the greatest Greco-Roman influence with many of the statuary during this period having idealized features.

Egyptian architecture was incredibly precise. The Egyptians did not have mortar, and they had no access to concrete, unlike the Romans. As such, their buildings had to be expertly designed, and their bricks had to fit snugly together. The most common materials for construction were limestone and sandstone.

Poor Egyptians were very similar to their European counterparts in terms of their dietary staples. The average person would consume copious amounts of bread and beer, with limited quantities of fish, various vegetables, and meats. Most of the poor were very malnourished.

Wealthier individuals had a heavily meat based diet, often sweetened with honey. The general exceptions to the lack of meat for the general population came with the hard laborers. Pyramid builders were fed an extensive amount of beef, in spite of how expensive this would have been. This may have been practiced due to the extreme physical exertion that would have come with building the pyramids. Workers would have to push and drag sandstone/limestone bricks up ramps. This was so physically intensive that it was not uncommon for several workers to die per day, either due to exhaustion of accidents.

The average Egyptian would have a very regimented day. As their taxes were so high, most farmers would have to begin their work as soon as they woke up in the morning and continued until the sun set at night. Their day would also be punctuated by their personal religious practices. The general public had little to no access to the temples, and thus would have to worship and honor their gods in their own personal home shrines. Average practice would include prayers and votive offerings to one's household and favorite deities.

8 MILITARY, TECHNOLOGY, MEDICINE, AND MATHMATICS

The military played an intensive role in Egyptian society from the Middle Kingdom until their eventual downfall at the hands of the Romans. Soldiers were afforded a place of honor in Egyptian society, though the outcome of battles were seen as either the will of the gods or the result of the cyclical nature of time.

The Egyptians were invaded multiple times by their neighbors, and were often under foreign rule for brief periods in their history. Foreign rulers included the Hyksos, Hittites, and eventually the Greeks in the form of the Ptomelic dynasty.

Egypt was a technologically advanced nation for the ancient world. They created architectural wonders that have been stated to be difficult even for modern people with much more advanced technological prowess. Though most buildings that the Egyptians made are no longer standing, the ones that are have truly stood the test of time and are not expected to fall to ruin any time soon.

The tools that the Egyptians used were largely made of stone. Bronze was not widely smelted in ancient Egypt, and this may have limited what they could have accomplished on a technological level.

They were, however, renowned shipbuilders. Their ships were mostly built for navigating the Nile River. However, there is some extremely limited evidence that they may have built ocean-worthy ships. Whether they ever made an Atlantic or Pacific crossing can only be speculated at this point in Egyptology. They were the first known shipbuilders to use stern mounted rudders.

Their glass working capabilities were famed throughout the Egyptian world. Where the ancient Celtic people were known for their goldsmithing, so too were the Egyptians known for their skill with glass. Colored glass was often used in trading with their neighbors.

Due to the flooding of the Nile on a yearly basis, the Egyptians did not develop extensive irrigation systems like their cousins in Europe or even other parts of Africa had to.

Like the Mayans, the Egyptians had an extensive knowledge of astronomy. Their liturgical calendar was lunar based and relied heavily on accurate calculations of the solstices and equinoxes. Many Egyptian monuments, including the great Pyramids of Giza, are aligned directly to astrological phenomenon. Interesting, the pyramids of the Mayans and the Aztecs are also aligned to such phenomenon, indicating a possible religious importance.

The Egyptians had the wheel, like many other cradles of civilization, and were capable of developing their own furniture. They favored couches and settees, but were known to sleep on beds made purely of stone.

There are fringe theories that suggest that the Egyptians may have had extremely limited access to electric lights. This is highly controversial within the field of Egyptology and has limited evidence supporting it. The primary evidence to refute the claim is that is highly unlikely that they could have developed a safe and reliable source of electric power.

Medical knowledge was limited among the Egyptians and may have contributed to adverse side effects. Their standard test for pregnancy included urinating on barley to see whether or not it sprouted. This does not indicate whether or not a woman is actually pregnant, and was little better than guesswork. The Egyptians would attempt to treat wounds by rubbing animal feces in them. This would quickly lead to infection, tetanus, and possibly even death. They had no knowledge of surgery, and could only perform rudimentary amputations. Zero knowledge of dentistry existed, and many mummies have been found with horrifically abscessed teeth which directly contributed to their deaths via sepsis.
Anatomical knowledge was limited, and only came about as a consequence of Egyptian funerary practices.

9 POPULATION

The population of ancient Egypt was comprised of ethnic Egyptians. Craniofacial studies of Egyptian mummies have spurred a considerable and controversial debate as to what race the Egyptian people were and whether or not the ancient Egyptians and the modern Egyptians are the same individuals on a genetic level. Studies have pointed to the Egyptians being a Mediterranean people, with traits more similar to those of the Romans, Greeks, and Indians. Some art from the early Christian period seems to corroborate this viewpoint. However, craniofacial data alone may be insufficient to determine what race the Egyptian people were, and most potential genetic samples have been compromised due to poor handling during the 19th and early 20th century.

Modern Egyptians do bear similarities to their ancient counterparts, however on a genetic level also bear similarities to the peoples of the Levant and of Nubia. It should be noted that the Egyptians of the New Kingdom and into the Islamic conquests had extensive contact with these populations.

The overall Egyptian population fluctuated over the Kingdom's history due to a variety of factors. Most of these population drops stemmed from famine, civil war, and outside military excursions. The 4.2 Kiloyear event caused a worldwide drought, which effected the yearly floods of the Nile River. This drought caused the utter collapse of the Old Kingdom in Egypt, and a 200 year long intermediate period. The resulting famines dropped the population of Egypt dramatically and led to the complete destabilization of the   region.

The Middle Kingdom was also marked by population growth that soon outstripped the land's capacity to feed everyone. The resulting famine, coupled with political instability due to a lack of a suitable heir to the throne, led to the collapse of the Middle Kingdom and the start of a second intermediate period marked by even more warfare, famine, and strife.

The end of ancient Egypt came about under foreign rule. The Ptolemaic dynasty was of Greek extraction, and had named themselves the Pharaohs in their own right in order to gain the respect of the population. The Hellenistic Egyptians adopted Egyptian culture, religion, and the practice of incestuous marriage. However, the Ptolemy's were known to abuse the religion of the Egyptians for their own benefit. Their reign was marked by frequent civil uprisings, famine, and strife. After the death of Cleopatra, it was relatively easy for the Romans to annex the politically and socially destabilized region. Though her son briefly claimed the throne and was recognized by some Egyptians as the legitimate Pharaoh, he was quickly assassinated. With his death came the end of a great civilization.

The Egyptians after this period were allowed to practice their faith as a Roman province up until the 5th century. The Romans were even willing to adopt Egyptian deities, most notably Isis. They were quickly Christianized, and became a center of Christianity. Later on, the nation was conquered by Islamic armies and remained over 85% Muslim to this day.

10 THE ULTIMATE LEGACY OF EGYPT

The Egyptians were one situation of many to have fallen. Though their fall occurred more than two thousand years ago, their legacy continues to permeate our lives to this very day.

During the 1800's, the world developed a renewed fascination with the ancient Egyptians in a style similar to their fascination with Greece and Rome during the Renaissance. Archaeologists descended upon Egypt, determined to learn everything that they could about these mysterious ancient people. The majority of these early Egyptologists were of British and French origin.

Unfortunately, these early Egyptologists did not have a great deal of respect for the Egyptian people. The vast majority of the discoveries made during the 1800 and into the early 1900's were taken out of Egypt, to be displayed in museums in Europe and America. Some artifacts, including the mummies of Pharaohs, were given to private collectors. Even worse, it became a brief craze to grind up and consume mummies, as it was believed to convey a general health benefit.

Egyptology during this period led to a renewed interest in racial differences. The debate as to what race the Egyptians were rages to this day, and is a highly controversial discussion in the field.

Egyptian religion, interestingly, continues in some forms to this day. The Coptic language, a daughter language of ancient Egyptian, is used for liturgical purposes in the Coptic Orthodox Churches. The Coptic Orthodox view themselves as the successors to Egyptian religion, and as the ones with the greatest claim to the culture of Egypt. This movement within the Coptic church is known as Pharaonism.

Judaism and Christianity have always held deep connections to the ancient Egyptians. The genesis of the Jewish people was said to take place in Egypt during the biblical exodus narrative. Until the rise of modern archaeology, this story was taken to be a literal history of the Jews in Egypt. Christianity later reaffirmed these ties through their tales surrounding the holy family's flight to Egypt, and Jesus Christ's alleged childhood within the nation. Egypt as a nation later became a thriving center of Christianity, along with the source of many of the controversies of the early church including the Arian controversy.

Egyptian religion is not limited by any means to forms of Christianity and Islam. Ancient Egyptian religion, along with other ancient polytheisms, saw a revival during the 20th century. Kemeticism, also known as Egyptian neopaganism, seeks to revive Egyptian faith and religion in its traditional context. Within the pagan world, there remains a debate between orthodox, polytheistic Kemetics and neo-Atenists, or those who seek to revive the cult of Aten. The Temple of Set is a loosely related religious organization, but only in as much as they worship the Egyptian god Seth. Theologically they remain closer to modern theistic Satanism.

The pantheon of the Egyptians had a tremendous influence on the pagan and occult movements of the 20th century, with the majority of organizations having some influence from Hermeticism or the Hermetic Order of the Golden Dawn.

Modern pop culture has drawn a tremendous amount of inspiration from Egyptian culture. The idea of the mummy and the curses that were placed on the tombs of Pharaohs has fascinated audiences for nearly 100 years. Films such as The Mummy with Boris Karloff and even Indiana Jones have drawn inspiration from the numerous treasures and horrors found within the tombs.

The tombs themselves have even become the subject of urban legend and superstition. The tomb of the boy King Tutankhamen is widely believed to have been cursed – a belief corroborated by the fact that its discoverers mysteriously died after having been inside of the tomb. The belief in the curse extends to the objects found within the tomb and Tutankhamen's mummy, with some museums changing their protocol in order to accommodate the superstition.

The architectural style of the Egyptians directly inspired later American monuments. The Washington Monument in Washington DC, the nation's capital, is directly based off of an Egyptian obelisk. The Luxor Hotel in Las Vegas, Nevada, is based off of both the Sphinx and the Pyramids. Both of these modern constructions have become monuments and national landmarks in their own right. It can be argued that while they are entirely based off the architecture of a prior civilization that they have become an integral part of Americana. Egyptian architecture exists right alongside revivalist Grecian and Roman architecture, and is an indispensable component of the architectural history of the Americas.

It can be argued that while Egypt itself had little to do with the West until it ultimately fell at the feet of Rome, that it was a cradle of Western civilization. Had it not been for the Egyptians, the field of archaeology would have been held back significantly. The Egyptomania craze of the 1800's renewed our collective interest in the past. While some of the actions taken by these early scientists were certainly regrettable, they developed the field leaps and bounds ahead of where it was. From early Egyptology was birthed modern archaeology. The discipline was born in the chaos and obsession fermenting among Europeans who were fascinated with a past that was foreign to them and the promise of treasures beyond their wildest dreams.

Even in the modern day, Egypt and the ancient Egyptian people are viewed with fascination. The mysticism inherent in their faith, their great architectural feats, and the relative obscurity they enjoyed until the modern era all serve to entrench them firmly in our collective imaginations. Their influence is sure to continue long into the future on both a religious and social level.

DUSTIN YARC

CONCLUSION

Thanks for making it through to the end of Egyptian Mythology. Let's hope it was informative and able to provide you with the information that you were looking for.

I hope you enjoyed learning about the vast information that surrounds the ancient Egyptian belief system and history of ancient Egypt, even if some of it is sparse and incomplete.

Finally, if you found this book useful in any way, a review on Amazon is always appreciated!

ABOUT THE AUTHOR

Dustin Yarc is an ambitious Canadian author who writes passionately about his hobbies and areas of expertise such as personal development, spirituality, video games, gardening, and cryptocurrencies. He self-published his first title at the age of eighteen.